YOU CHOOSE
BOOKS™

WORLD WAR II
NAVAL FORCES

An Interactive History Adventure

by Elizabeth Raum

Consultant:
Dennis Showalter, PhD
Professor of History
Colorado College

CAPSTONE PRESS
a capstone imprint

You Choose Books are published by Capstone Press,
1710 Roe Crest Drive, North Mankato, Minnesota 56003
www.capstonepub.com

Library of Congress Cataloging-in-Publication Data
Raum, Elizabeth.
  World War II naval forces : an interactive history adventure / by Elizabeth Raum.
    p. cm. — (You choose books. World War II)
  Includes bibliographical references and index.
  Summary: "Describes the role sailors played during World War II. Readers' choices
reveal various historical details"—Provided by publisher.
  ISBN 978-1-4296-4780-9 (library binding)
  ISBN 978-1-62065-720-1 (paperback)
  ISBN 978-1-4765-1812-1 (ebook PDF)
1. World War, 1939–1945—Naval operations—Juvenile literature. 2. Sailors—
History—20th century. I. Title.
  D770.R29 2013
  940.54′5—dc23   2012036764

Editorial Credits
Kristen Mohn, editor; Bobbie Nuytten, designer; Wanda Winch, media researcher;
Jennifer Walker, production specialist

Printed in the United States of America in Brainerd, Minnesota.
092012   006938BANGS13

TABLE OF CONTENTS

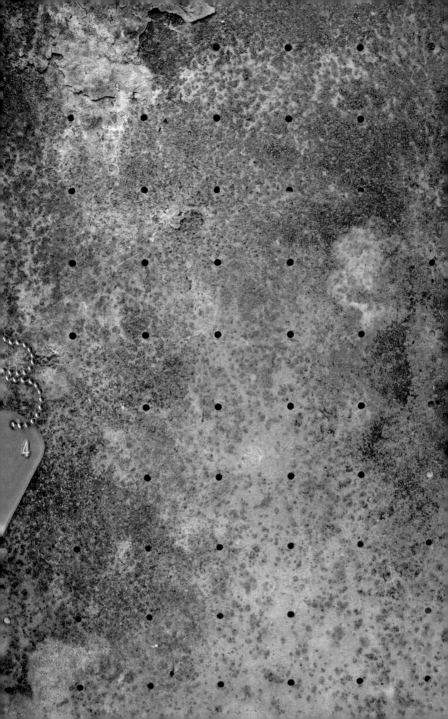

ABOUT YOUR ADVENTURE

YOU are living in a world on the brink of war. The Second World War is about to begin. Will you join in?

In this book you'll explore how the choices people made meant the difference between life and death. The events you'll experience happened to real people.

Chapter One sets the scene. Then you choose which path to read. Follow the directions at the bottom of each page. The choices you make will change your outcome. After you finish your path, go back and read the others for new perspectives and more adventures.

*YOU CHOOSE the path
you take through history.*

5

ATLANTIC OCEAN

NORWAY SWEDEN FINLAND

Gulf of Finland L. Ladoga *Rybinsk Res.*

North Sea DENMARK ESTONIA *Kuybyshev Res.*

IRELAND LATVIA S O V I E T   U N I O N

Baltic Sea LITHUANIA

U. K. NETH. EAST PRUSSIA

BELGIUM GERMANY POLAND

Bay of Biscay SWITZERLAND SLOVAKIA

HUNGARY

FRANCE ITALY *Adriatic Sea* ROMANIA *Black Sea*

PORTUGAL YUGOSLAVIA BULGARIA

SPAIN *Tyrrhenian Sea* GREECE *Aegean Sea* TURKEY

TUNISIA CYPRUS LEBANON SYRIA

EUROPE

☐ ALLIED CONTROLLED   ☐ AXIS CONTROLLED   ☐ NEUTRAL NATIONS

ASIA

SOVIET UNION

MONGOLIA MANCHURIA

PACIFIC OCEAN

KOREA

CHINA JAPAN

TIBET

NEPAL BHUTAN # WORLD WAR II, ALLIED AND AXIS TERRITORIES IN EUROPE AND ASIA

BURMA

BANGLADESH

INDIA THAILAND VIETNAM PHILIPPINES

FRENCH INDOCHINA

SRI LANKA

BRUNEI

MALAYSIA

SINGAPORE BORNEO

SUMATRA

NETHERLANDS INDIES NEW GUINEA

JOINING THE NAVY

Dad shakes his head as he puts the newspaper down. "I'm afraid we're headed for war again," he says. "Your uncle died on a battlefield in France in 1917. That war was supposed to be the 'war to end all wars.'"

"What makes you think there will be another?" you ask.

"The paper reports that Adolf Hitler just passed a law requiring all German men to serve in the army. He must be planning for war."

"With luck, any fighting will be over by the time you turn 18," Mother says.

"That's years from now," you say. But you think that fighting a war sounds exciting.

7

Turn the page.

You begin following the news in the papers, just like your dad does. Germany is not alone in preparing for war. In 1936 Italy and Japan join with Germany to form the Axis Powers. Italy, under its dictator, Benito Mussolini, wages war in Africa. In Asia, Japan is invading China.

In 1938 you read about the German Army's march into Austria. The next September you hear that 1.5 million German troops attacked Poland and claimed that nation for Germany.

Britain and France declare war on Germany. They call themselves the Allies. Australia, New Zealand, Canada, India, and South Africa join the Allies. Later the United States and the Soviet Union will become Allies too.

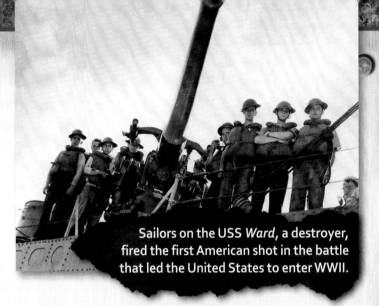

Sailors on the USS *Ward*, a destroyer, fired the first American shot in the battle that led the United States to enter WWII.

After the defeat of Austria and Poland, German troops invade Belgium, Norway, France, and the Netherlands. France falls to the Germans on June 22, 1940. Then Hitler turns his attention toward Great Britain.

By now you're old enough to think about enlisting in the military. Dad and Mother worry, but you've already decided that you'll join a naval force. The sea has always fascinated you. Imagine seeing the world from the deck of a huge ship!

Turn the page.

You read about the world's navies. Great Britain is already using its navy to protect merchant ships bringing supplies from North America to Europe. The advancing German Army has cut off supplies from Europe. Much of Great Britain's food, medical supplies, and military supplies are now shipped from Canada and the United States. Keeping the shipping lanes open across the Atlantic Ocean is necessary for Great Britain's survival.

Shutting down that supply route is Germany's goal. Germany uses submarines called U-boats to attack the merchant ships. In the first few months of 1940, German U-boats sank 110 merchant ships. Germany is also building large battleships.

Meanwhile, the U.S. Pacific fleet remains anchored in Pearl Harbor, Hawaii. So far the United States is not involved in the war.

The world's navies will play a major role in the war. Whether they serve on battleships, submarines, or landing crafts, navy members will be in the middle of the action.

• To serve as a sailor on the German battleship Bismarck, turn to page 13.

• To experience the Japanese attack on Pearl Harbor as a U.S. Marine, turn to page 41.

• To serve in the U.S. Navy during the D-Day invasion, turn to page 73.

11

The battleship *Bismarck* (below) and its sister ship, *Tirpitz*, were the biggest battleships Germany ever built.

CHAPTER 2

SINK THE *BISMARCK*!

Soon after you turn 18, you and your friend Hans join the Kriegsmarine, Germany's navy. After basic training you're assigned to the *Bismarck*, the biggest battleship in the world. It's bigger than the HMS *Hood*, Great Britain's most famous World War I battleship.

"The *Bismarck* is newer and more powerful," you tell Hans. "If the *Bismarck* ever battles the *Hood*, the *Bismarck* will win."

Hans smiles. "Of course!"

The *Bismarck* will be home to more than 2,000 men. They will need cooks, barbers, tailors, and doctors, as well as deckhands. You happen to mention that your father is a barber.

13

Turn the page.

"The ship needs a good barber," your commanding officer says. But Hans wants you to be a deckhand like him.

You'd get to spend your days outdoors as a deckhand. But being a barber might give you a chance to interact with the officers.

• To serve as a deckhand, go to page 15.

• To serve as a barber, turn to page 17.

You choose to work on deck. You report to the dock in Gdynia, Poland, in early April 1941. The *Bismarck* looms before you like a great gray whale. The ship is more than 800 feet long. Steel armor covers every visible surface. It looks indestructible.

Lieutenant Engel gives you your assignments. You'll scrub the decks and maintain the life rafts. And you'll handle the lines that connect the ship to the dock.

The ship has four big gun turrets. Each one holds two 15-inch guns. They're the biggest guns ever mounted on a German battleship. You will assist the gunnery crew at one of the turrets.

"This is your battle station. Whenever the alarm sounds, you are to report to this turret immediately," Engel says sternly.

Turn the page.

On May 18 the *Bismarck* pulls away from the wharf. The *Prinz Eugen*, a smaller, faster ship, will escort you on the mission. After two days at sea, the *Bismarck*'s commander, Captain Ernst Lindemann, says, "We're heading to the Atlantic. Our goal is to sink ships carrying supplies to Great Britain." It's a secret mission—and an important one.

Now that you're in the North Sea, Captain Lindemann orders four-hour watches. You stay on deck for four hours, sleep for four, and then return to watch. After a day or two, you're exhausted. You are sleeping soundly when the alarm bells sound. Is it part of your dream?

• *To go to your battle station, turn to page 22.*

• *To ignore the alarm, turn to page 24.*

"My son, a navy barber!" Dad says proudly.

"And you'll be safe below deck," Mother adds.

The ship is huge, but space for sleeping, eating, and haircutting is tight. The *Bismarck* is made for battle, not convenience. You're assigned a battle station near one of the gun turrets. "We'll need every hand on deck during a battle," your commander says.

Many officers confide in you as you cut their hair. In early March 1941 one of them says, "Chancellor Hitler plans to visit. Imagine that—our great leader on board the *Bismarck*."

Deckhands scrub the decks, laundry workers press uniforms, and you work overtime making the officers look their best. You put on your dress uniform and line up with the crew.

17

Turn the page.

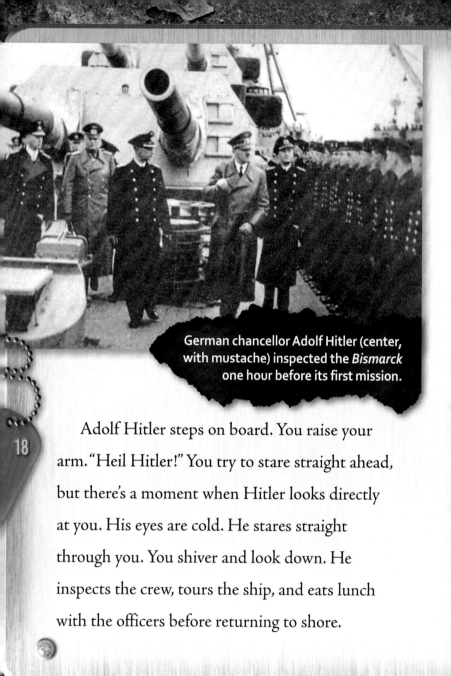

German chancellor Adolf Hitler (center, with mustache) inspected the *Bismarck* one hour before its first mission.

Adolf Hitler steps on board. You raise your arm. "Heil Hitler!" You try to stare straight ahead, but there's a moment when Hitler looks directly at you. His eyes are cold. He stares straight through you. You shiver and look down. He inspects the crew, tours the ship, and eats lunch with the officers before returning to shore.

On May 18 the *Bismarck* leaves dock. A few days later you notice that the big swastikas on the deck have been painted over. "We don't want enemy airplanes to know we are German," an officer explains. "We're going to the Atlantic to sink merchant ships carrying supplies from North America to Great Britain. Without supplies the British are sure to give up."

The ship's alarm sounds at 4:11 p.m. on May 23. You scramble up the ladder to your battle station. "False alarm," a sailor reports. The cold wind and heavy fog have put everyone on edge.

The alarm sounds again an hour later. You are cleaning the barbershop. An officer suggests you finish up. "It's probably another false alarm," he says.

19

• To report to your battle station, turn to page 20.

• To finish cleaning up, turn to page 26.

"I don't think it's a false alarm," you say. You race up the ladder toward your battle station. The deck is slippery with ocean spray. You are running too fast. You slide across the sea-soaked deck and slam into one of the big metal gun turrets. "My leg!" you shout before blacking out.

You awaken in the sick bay. A medic says, "You broke your leg. You've been unconcious for hours."

Hans stops by for a quick visit. "We sunk the *Hood!*" he tells you. "Now the British are after us. We're leaking oil and taking on water."

Hans hurries back to his battle station. The crew is on constant watch. No one has time to eat or sleep. The alarm sounds again and again, but you're stuck in bed.

The seas are rough. Seasick sailors report to the sick bay. They are sent back to their stations after a brief rest. Around noon a message comes over the loudspeakers:

"Seamen of the battleship *Bismarck*! We will fight until our gun barrels glow red-hot and the last shell has left the barrels. For us seamen, the question now is victory or death."

You drift to sleep and wake to a nightmare. Guns roar. The ship quakes. British bullets rain down on the metal deck above.

You want to help. When the ship rolls to the side, a closet door swings open. Medical supplies scatter. Several crutches land nearby.

• To get out of bed, turn to page 31.

• To stay in bed, turn to page 32.

You grab your life jacket and head for your battle station. Guns flash in the distance. "There's a ship heading our way, and it's firing!" a seaman shouts. The first salvo from the enemy splashes harmlessly into the ocean.

"The *Hood*—it's the *Hood*!" an officer shouts.

The gunnery commander waits until the ship is within firing range. Finally you hear the words "Permission to fire!" The roar is deafening. You put your hands up to cover your ears. Thick smoke chokes and blinds you.

"She's blowing up!" the officer shouts. Eight minutes into the battle, the *Hood* explodes and sinks. You and your mates cheer. You've sunk the mighty *Hood*!

However, the *Bismarck* has not escaped unharmed. Water is pouring in through a hole in the hull. Oil is leaking out. But the *Bismarck* speeds forward—other British ships may be chasing it.

Ever since the *Bismarck* reached the open waters of the Atlantic Ocean, Captain Lindemann has required the crew to be on constant watch. During one especially sleepy shift, your replacement shows up early. He offers to take over. You're hungry and so is the crew. Maybe you should go to the canteen for some food and bring something back to the others.

23

• To finish your shift, turn to page 27.

• To go to the canteen, turn to page 38.

Hans shakes you awake. "It's not a drill!" You throw on your clothes and climb topside to your battle station. Five minutes later, at 5:52 a.m., the British begin firing.

"It's the *Hood*!" an officer shouts. The enemy ship's guns are aimed at the *Bismarck*. But its first salvos fall short.

An officer shouts, "Permission to fire!" When the guns go off, it's like standing next to an exploding bomb. It's so noisy that your teeth rattle.

"She's blowing up!" Flames cover the *Hood*, and within seconds, she sinks.

You cheer. "We did it!" you yell. Then you realize that the British ship was filled with sailors just like you. "It could have been us," you say.

"But it wasn't," Hans replies.

HMS *Hood*, the Royal Navy's largest warship, was sunk during a battle with the *Bismarck*, killing more than 1,400 British sailors.

Captain Lindemann orders continuous watch. "The British are chasing us," Lieutenant Engel confides. Your four-hour watch is over. You are ready to drop with exhaustion. "Will someone go to the canteen to get food for the crew?" Engel asks. You need a nap more than food, but your crewmates do look hungry.

• To take a nap, turn to page 29.

• To go get food, turn to page 38.

You stay below to clean up. But this time the fight is real. It only lasts for 8 minutes. The crew of the *Bismarck* has blown the HMS *Hood* to bits. "We did it!" Hans yells. You cheer along with him.

"Our rudders have been damaged," Captain Lindemann says a few hours later. "We're going to France for repairs."

As you steam toward France, British planes buzz overhead. Guns boom constantly. A torpedo slams into the deck. Alarms sound on the morning of May 27. You report to your battle station. Strong winds whip around you. Rain pelts your face. "Two British ships," Hans says. "Maybe three. They want revenge."

"The ship is burning!" someone yells. "Save yourselves!" Some men are jumping overboard. Wait! Where did Hans go?

• To save yourself, turn to page 33.

• To find Hans, turn to page 37.

"I'll finish my shift," you tell your replacement. British torpedo planes buzz overhead. "Fire!" your commander orders. The planes fly away, but before long, they're back.

A torpedo slams into the starboard side of the deck, opposite your turret. The blast kills one seaman and damages the ship's boiler. Your hands shake and your heart thuds with each blast. No place is safe in war.

You fire and reload endlessly, losing track of time. Sometime later the admiral's voice comes over the loudspeaker. You only catch his final words: "For us seamen, the question now is victory or death." The words frighten you.

Turn the page.

You stay by the turret all night. Gunfire lights up the night sky. By the next day you're exhausted. Four hours of sleep is not enough. You're not the only one who falls asleep standing up.

Toward morning someone yells, "British ships!" The final battle has begun. "It's the *Rodney!*" a sailor yells. "And the *King George V*," says another. Shells batter the *Bismarck*'s deck. A fire begins burning nearby. Soon the entire ship is on fire. "Abandon ship!" an officer orders.

You run to the battery deck where the guns are mounted. Men are tossing inflatable life rafts into the sea. "Jump!" a sailor yells. It's a long way down, and you're not a strong swimmer.

28

• *To jump, turn to page 36.*

• *To look for a life jacket, turn to page 39.*

You're too tired to eat. You hurry to your quarters and crawl into your hammock. You're barely asleep when the alarm bells begin ringing. There's a deafening blast. The ship shudders and seems to scream. You leap out of your hammock and throw on your life jacket. "We've been hit!" an officer yells. "Get out! Get out now! Follow me!"

British ships and aircraft pursued and attacked the *Bismarck*, avenging the loss of the *Hood*.

Turn the page.

He leads you to a narrow tube that goes topside—to the deck surface. "Climb!" he shouts.

You remove your life jacket to fit inside. You pull yourself up the ladder, climbing as quickly as you can toward the light at the top. Several times your shirt snags, and you stop to pull it free.

You tumble onto the deck into thick smoke. A British shell hits the deck and splinters into dozens of deadly fragments.

Men leap into the ocean. You're afraid to follow them into the thrashing waves without your life jacket. You look around desperately, wondering what to do.

• To look for a life raft, turn to page 33.

• To find a life jacket, turn to page 39.

You reach for a crutch and stand up. You hobble to the door of the sick bay. You are almost there when the ship lurches and tosses you onto the metal floor. Your head slams into a steel support.

When a medic rushes back to the sick bay for supplies, he finds your lifeless body curled against a metal locker. You won't be the only sailor to die on the *Bismarck* today.

THE END
To follow another path, turn to page 11.
To read the conclusion, turn to page 101.

The ship rocks back and forth. If you try to get up now, you're certain to fall. There's one explosion after another as the main guns blast the British ships. The British fire back. "The *Bismarck* is unsinkable," you tell yourself, but you're no longer sure you believe it. Smoke fills the sick bay. You try to sit up, but you're dizzy. You pull the blankets over your head to block the smoke.

In the engine room, Chief Engineer Walter Lehmann knows the ship can't be saved. He orders his men to sink the *Bismarck* by opening valves to let water into the hull. "It is better to sink our own ship than to let it fall into enemy hands." And so, amid a hail of British bombs and torpedoes, the mighty battleship slides into the ocean. You and hundreds of sailors die with her.

THE END

To follow another path, turn to page 11.
To read the conclusion, turn to page 101.

32

You turn to run, but the ship is tipping. The deck tilts under your feet and you slide toward the edge. You plunge feetfirst into the icy water.

"Ahh!" you scream, struggling to catch your breath. Your legs and feet are numb with cold. As you thrash in the water, the British cruiser *Dorsetshire* steams toward you. British sailors lower ropes over the side. You begin pulling yourself up the rope, right into the hands of the British. They drag you over the railing, strip off your oil-soaked clothes, and wrap you in blankets.

You're surprised when they offer you hot tea and biscuits. These men are your enemies. Why are they being kind? Would you do the same for them?

33

Turn the page.

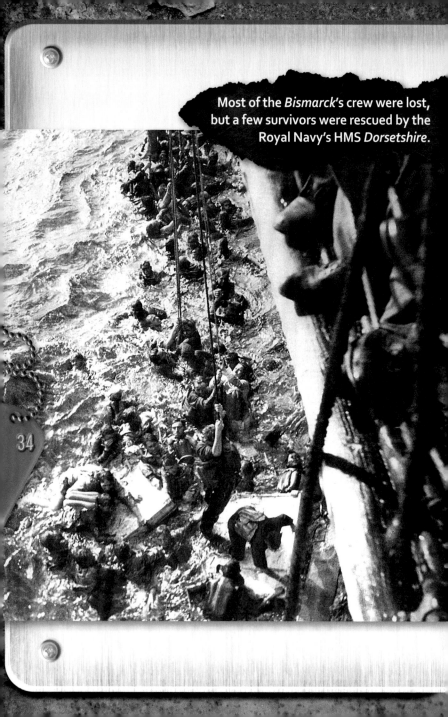

Most of the *Bismarck*'s crew were lost, but a few survivors were rescued by the Royal Navy's HMS *Dorsetshire*.

34

The *Dorsetshire* sails away with you aboard, leaving hundreds of German sailors in the water. A British sailor explains that German U-boats are nearby. You're relieved. Maybe the U-boats will save the others.

Eventually you are sent to a prisoner of war camp in Canada. When you return to Germany after the war, you take over your father's barbershop. You never return to the sea.

Years pass before you find Hans again. He'd been taken to a different camp. You are the lucky ones. Few of the *Bismarck*'s crew survived. You seldom talk about the war. There are too many sad memories.

35

THE END
To follow another path, turn to page 11.
To read the conclusion, turn to page 101.

Luck is with you. You shoot to the surface next to a life raft. A sailor helps you into the raft. You turn to look at the *Bismarck*. Flames dance along the deck. Some sailors jump into the sea. Others stand still, dazed and overwhelmed. The ship begins to tilt, and then the mighty *Bismarck* disappears into the sea. You can't believe it.

All day long your raft bobs on the waves. At 7:00 p.m. a German U-boat comes along. The sailors aboard pull you to safety. The sub searches for other survivors but finds none. You later learn that of the 2,206 men who sailed on the *Bismarck*, German ships rescued only five.

Every year on May 27, you salute the brave men who died on the *Bismarck*.

THE END

To follow another path, turn to page 11.
To read the conclusion, turn to page 101.

There's Hans! You both slide down the starboard hull to the keel and jump from there. "Swim!" he yells. "There's a British ship. They won't leave us here to drown."

That's when another sailor reaches out and grabs your life jacket. "Help me!" he says. "I can't swim!" He pulls you under.

"Let go!" you yell, but he holds even tighter. He thrashes around and pushes your head under the icy water. You struggle, but it's no use. You drown just a few yards from the British ship that rescues Hans.

37

THE END

To follow another path, turn to page 11.
To read the conclusion, turn to page 101.

It won't take long to go to the canteen for some hot food before you crawl into your bunk. "I'll bring you coffee too," you promise.

You're on your way to the canteen when a British plane flies over. Your mates begin firing their guns, but they aren't fast enough. The plane releases a torpedo. It slams into the hull right beside you. The blast throws you against a metal wall, snapping your neck. You become the first sailor to die on the battleship *Bismarck*. You won't be the last.

38

THE END

To follow another path, turn to page 11.
To read the conclusion, turn to page 101.

You run to get a life jacket. They're in a storage locker at the front of the ship. Devastation is everywhere. Fires burn along the length of the deck. The turrets are silent wrecks. But seeing the injured men is far worse. Some are missing legs or arms. Others hold their bleeding hands over gaping wounds.

A man reaches out for you. "Tell my girl I love her," he pleads just as a British shell slams into the deck. The blast knocks you down. A metal splinter pierces your neck. You die quickly with no time to think of the loved ones you're leaving behind.

39

THE END

To follow another path, turn to page 11.
To read the conclusion, turn to page 101.

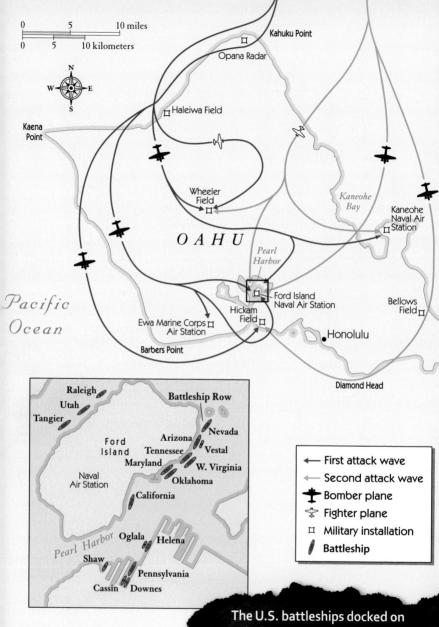

0 5 10 miles		
0 5 10 kilometers		

Kahuku Point

Opana Radar

Haleiwa Field

Kaena Point

Wheeler Field

Kaneohe Bay

Kaneohe Naval Air Station

O A H U

Pearl Harbor

Ford Island Naval Air Station

Bellows Field

Pacific Ocean

Ewa Marine Corps Air Station

Hickam Field

Honolulu

Barbers Point

Diamond Head

Raleigh

Utah

Tangier

Battleship Row

Nevada

Arizona

Tennessee

Vestal

Ford Island

Maryland

W. Virginia

Naval Air Station

Oklahoma

California

Pearl Harbor

Oglala

Helena

Shaw

Pennsylvania

Cassin   Downes

←	First attack wave
←	Second attack wave
✈	Bomber plane
✈	Fighter plane
☐	Military installation
⬮	Battleship

The U.S. battleships docked on Battleship Row were the primary targets of the Japanese raid.

CHAPTER 3

SURPRISE ATTACK

"I want to be a leatherneck," you tell your mother.

"A leatherneck?" she says, looking concerned.

"A United States Marine," you say proudly.

Before long it's time to leave for boot camp. It's tough saying goodbye. Mom cries and Dad hugs her. They both wave as you board the bus to San Diego, California.

Boot camp lasts seven weeks. You spend most of your time in close order drill. You learn to march, take and give orders, and handle a rifle. You also learn to set up camp and perform first-aid. You receive special training in how to guard important people and places.

41

Turn the page.

The drills are exhausting, the sergeant tough, and the beds uncomfortable. But by the end of boot camp you're ready to serve wherever and however you are needed.

In November 1941 you report to Pearl Harbor, Hawaii. It's the home base of the U.S. Navy's Pacific fleet. More than 90 ships are anchored there. Seven battleships line the southeast shore of Ford Island. "It's called Battleship Row," your buddy Jack says.

First in line is the *California*. Then several ships are moored side-by-side: *Maryland* with *Oklahoma*, and *Tennessee* with *West Virginia*. The *Arizona* is moored next to the repair ship *Vestal*. The *Nevada*, last in line, is all by herself. The eighth ship, the *Pennsylvania*, is in dry dock nearby for repairs.

You've always dreamed of serving on a battleship. You'll have the chance to sail the world. But if you work at the Marine base, you'll have the chance to explore Hawaii.

43

• To serve on a navy battleship, turn to page 44.

• To work at the Marine base, turn to page 48.

Eighty-seven Marines and nearly 1,500 sailors are assigned to the *Arizona*. You'll be guarding the brig, the gangplank, and other important areas of the ship. If there's a battle, you'll report to the superstructure deckhouse at the top of the ship. You'll man the 5-inch, 51-caliber guns that make up the secondary batteries.

For several weeks you practice battle drills at sea. On December 6 the *Arizona* returns to Pearl Harbor. On Sunday, December 7, you wake up early. As you're about to leave the breakfast table, the ship's siren for air defense sounds.

"We're being attacked!" a sailor yells.

You run to the port door in time to see a bomb strike a barge of some kind near the *Nevada*. Anti-aircraft guns fire back.

You climb the ladder on the starboard side of the ship near the tail. Your friend Harry follows. You scramble up another ladder to the second deck, past the Marines' compartment. One more ladder takes you above it and past one of the ship's casemates.

The casemate, an armored tower containing one of the ship's big guns, has a large window. It overlooks Ford Island and the battleship *Tennessee*. Harry stops to peer out. "Look!" he yells. "A Jap plane!"

You can see the Japanese flag on the underside of its wing. It drops something that looks oblong at first, and then becomes as round as a ball. It flashes into the sea about 100 yards from you. Whump! It's a bomb!

Turn the page.

Water splashes onto the deck. The ship lists 5 or 6 degrees toward the port side. You grab a railing to keep your balance. Did the bomb explode underwater? Did it damage the ship? You have no way to know. For the first time, the war feels real to you.

Ford Island had a navy yard for building and repairing ships, a naval air station, a hospital, and other facilities.

Another plane flies overhead. Boom! A torpedo strikes the ship. The *Arizona* rises out of the water. It then slams against the quay, the platform next to the ship for loading supplies. The impact sends men sprawling across the deck. The loudspeaker blares: "Japanese are attacking, all hands General Quarters." That means you have to get to your battle station in the main mast—now!

The *Arizona* has many decks and is as long as two football fields. But Harry stops at the bottom of the tripod mast leg because something is blocking his way. "It's Lieutenant Simonsen! He's been hit!" Harry kneels beside him.

• *To help Harry with the lieutenant, turn to page 51.*

• *To report to your battle station, turn to page 53.*

47

You're assigned to the Marine barracks at U.S. Navy headquarters. It's where the navy trains men for sea duty or to serve as guards at U.S. embassies around the world. You patrol the grounds, check identification papers, and do whatever it takes to keep order.

On December 6 you have liberty. You can do whatever you want. You decide to swim and surf at Waikiki Beach with your buddy Jack. It's great fun and an exciting change from life at home. Some sailors invite you to a luau. Beautiful girls dance the hula while musicians strum ukuleles. "This is the life," you say. "I could stay here forever."

"Too bad we have to be back on base by 11 o'clock," Jack says.

The next morning, December 7, you wake up at 7:00. "Why so early?" Jack asks, yawning.

"I promised my mother I'd go to church. So did you." You shower and shave. "Let's go. We'll get coffee and a doughnut on the way."

But you never make it off the base. A few minutes before 8:00, you hear an explosion. Bullets punch holes in the barracks roof. "We're under attack!" Sergeant Wilson yells, but you barely hear him over the drumming of the bullets and the panic of your mates.

"Attack? But the United States isn't at war!"

Several bombers fly overhead. The red circles under the wings represent the Japanese flag. You call them meatballs.

49

Turn the page.

"It's the Japs," Sarge says. "And they're headed for Battleship Row." That's where the navy's big battleships dock. You run down the hallway and grab a rifle from the gun rack. So does Jack.

Sarge leads you to a retaining wall that provides some cover. "When I give the command, fire!" What good is a rifle against a bomber? But before you can shoot, Sarge yells, "Hold your fire!"

A lone sailor is trying to set up a machine gun about 100 feet away. "That man needs help," Sarge yells. You'll have to cross an open patch of ground to reach him.

• To volunteer to help the sailor, turn to page 59.

• To stay with Sarge, turn to page 63.

50

You stop to help the lieutenant, but it's too late. He's dying. He motions for you to continue up the ladder.

You climb the ladders on the tripod mast to your battle station. Japanese machine gunners fire down on you. Bullets ping off the ship's metal armor and chip the paint around you.

A bomb hits the quarterdeck, creating a large hole. You reach your battle station, but there's not much you can do. Your guns are no use against the Japanese bombers.

51

Turn the page.

You look out over Ford Field, where navy planes smoke and burn. The sky is filled with Japanese planes bombing other battleships along Battleship Row. The shock of the attack silences the men around you.

Then a Japanese bomb crashes into the bow of the ship. It explodes in the powder magazine, setting off the ammunition stored there. The ship shakes, lurches, and rises out of the water before it explodes.

You're tossed onto the deck. The smell of burning oil wraps itself around you like a heavy blanket. You're tempted to take cover behind one of the ship's steel supports. But if you can get below, maybe you can reach the gangplank and escape.

• To go below, turn to page 55.

• To take cover, turn to page 56.

52

It's your job to get to your battle station. You are climbing toward it when you hear a loud whooshing sound. That sound is followed by a series of explosions. Torpedoes have hit the ship below water level.

All eight U.S. battleships at Pearl Harbor were either sunk or badly damaged.

53

Turn the page.

A bomb goes directly down one of the gun turrets. The powder magazine, where ammunition is stored, explodes. The *Arizona* shakes. Men tumble onto the deck. Smoke swirls around you. The ship—what's left of it—is on fire! The battle is less than 20 minutes old.

You begin climbing down the ladder toward the gangplank. You have to get off the ship! You're nearly there when a torpedo explodes on the battleship *Nevada*. The explosion makes the *Arizona* bounce around like a toy boat. An officer orders, "Abandon ship!"

But where's Harry? You need to get off the ship, but you can't leave your friend behind.

• To abandon ship, turn to page 57.

• To look for Harry, turn to page 71.

You go below. By the time you reach the quarterdeck, the heat is intense. Badly burned sailors move past you like zombies. Most are beyond help.

The ship's mooring lines pull tight against the weight of the sinking ship. In a few more minutes they'll break. The ship will go down. The gangplank has flipped sideways. To cross, you'll have to walk along a 2-inch-wide strip of plank to the quay, the platform used to load and unload supplies.

If you can get across, you'll be safe—at least for a while. You're about to step onto the plank when someone calls your name. Is it Harry?

• To turn around, turn to page 58.

• To keep going, turn to page 65.

You run along the deck. There's the gangplank! You're almost to safety. But the deck is slick with the blood of wounded men. As you race forward, you fall and slide toward the railing. You try to grab something—anything—but you keep sliding. Another bomb hits the ship. The next thing you know, you're in the water.

Navy sailors were able to rescue a few men from the water during the attacks.

56

Turn to page 61.

You make a dash for the steps leading belowdecks. You stumble down them and head for the gangplank. "Hurry!" a sailor says. "This gangplank is about to give way." It sways wildly as you cross to the quay.

The only way to shore from the quay is to swim. You dive into the chilly water and swim past globs of oil, pieces of metal and wood, and even dead bodies. Finally you climb ashore and collapse. Some men are crying. Others, like you, feel stunned and dazed as they watch the mighty battleships burn.

57

Turn to page 67.

"Harry?" you call, but you can't see him. Meanwhile, another Marine moves ahead of you. He's halfway across when a cable near the gangplank snaps. The jolt knocks the sailor into the water below.

"Let's go!" someone behind you yells. You hold your breath and force yourself across the gangplank to the quay.

Several small boats are moored there. Joe, one of the ship's carpenters, is trying to start a boat. But he seems confused. You don't know how to handle the boat either.

"Get in," he says. But it might be safer to swim.

• To swim ashore, turn to page 61.

• To get into the boat, turn to page 64.

"I'll go!" you shout. Jack goes too. Planes fly overhead, and bullets spray the dirt around you. You've never run so fast in your life. The machine gun sits next to an ammo shed. It offers little protection against the raining bullets. You and Jack help the sailor set up and load the gun.

"Hold it steady!" You aim the gun toward a bomber. Jack gives the command. "Ready, aim, fire!"

The Japanese bomber explodes. "That's one less meatball!" Jack yells.

Turn the page.

You fire until you're out of ammunition. That's when fear takes over. Your country may not be officially at war, but you're in the middle of a major battle. Your hands shake. You're excited and scared at the same time. Reading about war in the newspaper is different from living it.

The attack stops suddenly. Sergeant Wilson says, "Form two groups. One group will stay here and man the guns. The other will go to the dock to help the wounded."

• To help the wounded, turn to page 68.

• To man the guns, turn to page 70.

Crewmembers of the USS *California* fled from their burning ship.

Waves slap you in the face, choking you. Bits of steel and pieces of wood slosh past you in the choppy water. You see a buoy and grab onto it. Wave after wave of Japanese planes passes overhead, dropping bombs and spraying bullets. The sky lights up like a fireworks display. But it's not fireworks—it's the *Arizona*.

Turn the page.

All the ammunition, guns, and shells are exploding in a series of roars, pops, and booms. Oil and bits of twisted metal from the damaged ships float past.

For a while, the attack stops. You begin the mile-long swim to shore. By the time you get there, you're exhausted and covered with oil and sludge. Your uniform has turned black. So have your skin and hair. But you're safe. You survived.

Every year on December 7 you remember the 2,403 sailors and civilians who weren't as lucky. You'll never forget the sacrifice they made.

THE END

To follow another path, turn to page 11.
To read the conclusion, turn to page 101.

You hate to admit it, but you're scared. Even Sarge looks worried. Another man volunteers to help with the machine gun. You feel safer behind the retaining wall. When the next plane passes over, you aim for the red circle on the wing.

"Ready, aim, fire!" Sarge yells. You fire a rifle. Others shoot pistols as the machine gun rattles out bullets. The plane explodes. "Hurray! We got one!"

The bombing stops as quickly as it began. An officer sends you to guard the main gate at Marine headquarters. You hear explosions in the distance and sirens whining, but the worst seems to be over.

Turn to page 67.

The water is full of oil, sludge, and dead bodies. You can't imagine trying to swim through it, so you take a chance on the boat. But Joe is struggling to control the boat.

"Give me the wheel!" another man yells. A fight breaks out. When you stand up to stop the fight, you're knocked overboard. Your head smashes into a steel beam. You sink below the churning water, a victim of the surprise Japanese attack on Pearl Harbor.

THE END

To follow another path, turn to page 11.
To read the conclusion, turn to page 101.

You don't stop. You have to escape the burning ship. You're halfway across the gangplank when one of the heavy cables between the ship and the quay snaps. The jolt knocks you off the plank. You hit the side of the sinking ship with a thud. You slip beneath the surface of the water, unconscious. You'll be counted among the 2,403 who died in the attack on Pearl Harbor.

THE END

To follow another path, turn to page 11.
To read the conclusion, turn to page 101.

66

Air Force planes and hangars at nearby Hickam Field were also targeted by Japanese bombers.

You're shaken, but alive. You're assigned to the *Maryland* as a security officer. She was luckier than most of the ships on Battleship Row. Only two bombs hit the *Maryland*, causing light damage.

By February 1942 the ship returns to active service with you on board. You return home when the war ends in 1945, but you never forget what happened at Pearl Harbor on December 7, 1941.

THE END

To follow another path, turn to page 11.
To read the conclusion, turn to page 101.

You run to the water's edge. The men who jumped from the battleships are coated with oil and slime. Some are badly injured, burned, or missing limbs. You feel sick. You force down your fear and help them out of the water.

You pull several men to shore. An ambulance roars up. Medics whisk the men away. Many will not survive their injuries. More bodies float in the water. Pulling them out is the saddest thing you've ever done.

A second attack begins. Planes drop bombs and spray the ground with bullets. You look toward the battleships and see the great *Oklahoma* flop onto its side. The *Arizona* explodes.

The next three days pass in a blur. There's no time to do anything but follow orders. Finally you steal a minute to send a message home. Your telegram is just two words: "Am Safe." It's the best news your mother has ever received. She treasures it as long as she lives.

69

THE END

To follow another path, turn to page 11.
To read the conclusion, turn to page 101.

You and Jack man the machine gun. "Another attack may come at any moment," the sergeant says.

"We need more ammo," you say. You offer to dash across the open area to the shed where the ammunition is stored. As you run to the shed, another bomber flies over. This time you're the target. A bullet strikes you in the leg. You stumble and fall but are able to crawl to safety.

You're treated on the hospital ship *Solace* and then transferred to a military hospital on the mainland. For the rest of your life, you walk with a limp. But you consider yourself lucky. You made it home safely—unlike thousands of others who died in the attack on Pearl Harbor.

70

THE END

To follow another path, turn to page 11.
To read the conclusion, turn to page 101.

"Harry!" you call, but it's impossible to hear anything over the explosions. You zigzag past fires, debris, and injured men to the place where you last saw Harry. He's resting against a metal support. "Over here, pal," he calls. He's gripping his stomach, trying to stop the flow of blood.

"I took a hit," he says. "Will you write my mom? Tell her I love her."

You grab Harry under his arms. "I'll get you out of here."

But it's too late. Harry dies in your arms. Moments later a Japanese plane buzzes overhead, raining bullets onto the burning deck. One of them hits you. You collapse and die on the deck of the burning *Arizona* next to your pal Harry.

71

THE END

To follow another path, turn to page 11.
To read the conclusion, turn to page 101.

Navy sailors were briefed before beginning the D-Day invasion.

CHAPTER 4

INVASION

Mother's voice is shaking as she reads the headline out loud: "U.S. Declares War; Military Casualties Total Almost 2,500." She puts down the newspaper and shakes her head.

"I'm joining the navy," you say.

"Not until you graduate from high school," Mother insists.

For the next two years you read about the war, put battle maps on your bedroom wall, and talk to anyone who has ever served as a sailor. The day after high school graduation, you enlist in the navy.

73

Turn the page.

The navy barber shaves your head. It's called a buzz cut. You are issued a uniform, a hammock with a mattress and two blankets, and a seabag to carry it all.

They call you a "boot" and give you *The Bluejackets' Manual.* "Study it!" Chief Petty Officer Rogers says. But after a day of doing sit-ups, marching, and rifle training, you're too tired to do much reading.

One day Chief Rogers says, "We need men to serve in the amphibious force. You'll learn to handle an LCM, which is a landing craft, mechanized. It takes men and equipment from ship to shore." You like the sound of that, so you volunteer.

At the training center in Little Creek, Virginia, you're assigned to an LCM 6, a 56-foot steel boat. It takes four men to handle the LCM. The coxswain controls the boat and the motor mac repairs the engine. You and another bowman, Tom, stand watch to make sure the LCM doesn't hit any obstacles. There's no armor on the open deck to protect you from enemy bullets.

When your training is finished, you go to England to prepare for a secret landing in Europe. Everyone is excited. This is the big invasion you've been waiting for. If the landing goes well, the Allies can begin marching across Europe.

Turn the page.

On June 5, 1944, you receive orders to cross the English Channel to France. "In another 12 hours we'll send the troop carriers across," Captain Orr, one of the commanding officers, says. "We want the landing craft ready to take soldiers from ships to shore."

The sea is choppy. Waves 10 to 12 feet high rock the LCM. It's 5:30 a.m. when you reach the area 11 miles offshore where U.S. troop carriers are anchored. A boat officer directs you to pull alongside one of the carriers.

Eighty navy bomb experts board the LCM. The men fill every bit of space in the LCM. "It's like being packed in an open tin can," Tom says. Each man carries two packs of explosives. On shore they'll blow up the bridges and roads. That should stop the German Army!

Army troops crowded onto a landing craft headed to Normandy.

Turn the page.

You head for Omaha Beach. The beach is crowded with crafts trying to land. But you manage to drop off the troops and go back for a second load.

During the second trip, you are carrying a group of army infantrymen to shore. German snipers begin firing down at you from machine gun nests on the cliffs above! You have no weapons or protection in the open boat. Bullets pelt the deck. Your instincts tell you to cower and protect yourself, but that won't help.

You ignore the danger and do what you've been trained to do—get the troops to shore. But you think you see something just under the water ahead. You're the bowman. It's up to you to tell the coxswain to back off or push forward.

• To back off, go to page 79.

• To push forward, turn to page 80.

You give the "back off" signal to the coxswain. The Germans have rigged mines offshore to protect this 6-mile stretch of Omaha Beach from invasion. You recall the officer's warning: "Be alert. If you hit a mine, it will destroy the LCM and everyone on it."

Luckily this obstacle isn't a mine. It's an overturned tank that fell off a landing craft. The coxswain swerves to the right, and the LCM moves forward. But the conditions are getting worse. Fog and smoke from gunfire block your view. Waves rock the boat. The bullets keep coming. "We need to get these men ashore!" Lieutenant Johnson yells. "Lower the ramp!"

"But, sir, the water's too rough and deep," you reply.

• To lower the ramp, turn to page 81.

• To wait, turn to page 83.

The lieutenant in charge orders you forward. His men want to get to shore. But do they know that the Germans have planted explosives in the water? If you hit a mine, the LCM will be blown to bits.

You hold your breath as you continue forward. Then you sigh in relief. It's not a mine—just a tank that fell off a larger landing craft. You're safe, this time.

The troops plunge into the icy water and wade ashore. You're about to return to the ship for more troops when another landing craft loses control in the waves. It tips over. Men struggle in the deep water, weighed down by their gear. If you rescue them, you'll be a target for the German gunners firing from the bluff above.

• To rescue the men in the water, turn to page 85.

• To return to the ship, turn to page 86.

Lieutenant Johnson insists. You and Tom lower the ramp. Rough water forces the ramp to buck up and slam back down. The first man off can't get out of the way in time. The ramp smacks him in the head. "Ow!" he yells. "That could have killed me."

"Jump off the sides!" Johnson orders, leading the way. The men follow and begin wading through water reaching their armpits. One soldier is seasick. He throws up and drops his helmet.

"You can't go ashore without a helmet," you say, giving him yours. He salutes you as he jumps off the LCM. He may be an army man, but he's wearing a navy helmet when he storms Omaha Beach.

Turn the page.

Several men make it safely to shore. Others struggle against the waves. As you're backing up, you see a soldier who's having trouble staying afloat in the water. He's several feet below you. Reaching out to him will put you in danger, especially since you gave your helmet away.

Army troops waded to Omaha Beach from a landing craft.

• To help the man, turn to page 84.

• To keep going, turn to page 92.

"Give us a minute," you say. "If we can get in closer, you'll be safer." Lieutenant Johnson agrees. You lower the ramp a few feet closer to shore. The troops all make it off the LCM, but they have to duck German bullets on their way to shore. The water is full of wounded men. You rescue those within easy reach and take them back to the ships. The medics will help them.

When you return from your sixth run, Captain Orr directs you to a Liberty ship. Liberty ships carry supplies. They hold more than 9,000 tons of cargo. That equals 2,840 jeeps, 440 tanks, or 230 million rounds of rifle ammunition. Captain Bunker, the Liberty ship captain, greets you and invites you on board for a hot meal. But you have work to do.

• To accept a meal, turn to page 89.

• To return to duty, turn to page 94.

You reach out to the soldier with a pole. He grabs it and pulls so hard that you lose your balance and fall overboard. The water is littered with packs, guns, and clothing. Worst of all are the bodies of soldiers killed as they tried to make it to shore.

You can't find the soldier you were trying to help. You reach the shore and take cover behind an overturned tank. German bullets ping off of it.

A soldier a few feet from you is hit and tumbles backward. His rifle falls nearby. You can't help him, but you may be able to reach his gun. You glance out at the sea. Is that your LCM still in the landing zone?

• To run for the LCM, turn to page 87.

• To reach for the rifle, turn to page 91.

The overturned LCM is close to yours, so you call to the men. "Over here! We can help!" Several are able to swim within reach. You pull one soldier out of the water. Several of his buddies follow. Many are injured. The German guns are still firing. Without any weapons, you feel as if a big target is painted on the LCM's deck. You've stayed too long. Luckily most of the men have clambered aboard.

"Let's go!" you shout. You look over the side and see a dark shape beneath the water. It could be the LCM's shadow. Or it could be a German mine.

• To ignore the shadow, turn to page 95.

• To check for mines, turn to page 96.

Leaving those men in the water is one of the toughest things you've ever done. Tom senses your concern. "Some of them will make it on their own," he says. "And the more troops we transport, the better our chance of victory."

You carry troops and equipment ashore for two days. The battle has moved inland and the beach is secured. As you make a final landing, the LCM scrapes against an overturned tank and is damaged. The coxswain beaches the LCM. "This will take a while," the motor mac says. "You boys may as well have a look around."

You and Tom climb one of the cliffs. At the top you find a German "pillbox." It's a concrete shelter designed to hold a machine gun and several soldiers. There's a small steel door.

• To open the door, turn to page 98.

• To leave it alone, turn to page 99.

86

It is your LCM! You dodge bullets as you zigzag across the sand and swim toward it. The tide is coming in. The water pushes against you as you swim. You reach the LCM and climb on just before Tom closes the ramp.

"Thought we lost you," Tom says.

You take healthy soldiers to shore and wounded soldiers back to the ship all day long. You lose track of how many trips you've made before darkness makes it impossible to continue. By that time, you're exhausted.

The coxswain drops anchor far from the beach. You eat K rations and set up your cot on the deck of the LCM. You try to block the horrible images of the dead and wounded from your mind.

Turn the page.

An amphibious vehicle called an LST (landing ship, tank) unloaded British tanks and trucks for the attack.

88

You transport soldiers to the beach for two more days. When the troops move inland, your work eases up.

Turn to page 97.

A hot meal sounds great. The steaming plate of steak and eggs is the best food you've had in weeks. What's the catch?

You learn soon enough. The Liberty ship is loaded with ammunition. "We're setting up an ammo dump on the beach," Captain Bunker says. "Now that we've taken the beach, the army will begin the long march across France to Germany. They'll need plenty of ammo to fight the Germans." They begin loading up your LCM.

After the short trip to shore carrying the ammo, army troops unload the LCM. While they're working, you and your mates wander onto the bluffs. This is where German machine gunners fired down on you during the invasion. The machine gun nests are burned out, the guns silenced, and their operators killed in action.

89

Turn the page.

The beach is an Allied military post now. Jeeps, trucks, and tanks lumber along the sand. They'll carry supplies to the Allied armies. Your job here is done. Soon you'll be sent for more training. Then you'll head to the Pacific to assist with the invasion of Japanese-held islands.

There will be more battles, but it is this battle that you'll remember most clearly. You'll never forget the brave soldiers who stormed the beaches of Normandy on D-Day.

THE END
To follow another path, turn to page 11.
To read the conclusion, turn to page 101.

The rifle is so close. But you have to leave the safety of the overturned tank to grab it. You're only exposed to gunfire for a few seconds, but that's all it takes for a German bullet to strike your leg. You crawl back to the tank. You stay hidden for hours, clenching your teeth against the pain until a medic rescues you.

You spend the next few months in a navy hospital in Virginia. You follow the progress of the war, knowing that you helped the Allies to victory. You only wish you could have done more.

THE END

To follow another path, turn to page 11.
To read the conclusion, turn to page 101.

Lots of men are struggling. You'd like to help them all, but your job is to get more troops to shore. You speed back to the troop carrier. On your third trip to the beach, waves are so high that you can't get close enough to release the ramp. Finally an officer jumps over the side. "Let's go!" he orders. The men hold their guns over their heads and wade to shore. German bullets batter the LCM and strike men in the water. Two soldiers are hit as they jump off the LCM. You reach out and pull them back on board.

At the same moment, a bullet hits Tom. "Tom!" You rush forward, but Tom pushes you away. "I'm OK," he says. "The bullet only grazed me. I'm fine."

You turn to signal the coxswain, and that's when a bullet strikes you. But it doesn't just graze you—it pierces your chest and kills you instantly.

The LCM carries your body back to the troop carrier with the other dead and wounded. For you, the war is over.

LCMs carried dead and injured troops from the beaches back to the ships.

THE END

To follow another path, turn to page 11.
To read the conclusion, turn to page 101.

"Maybe later," you say. "We have to report to the boat director first." You make many trips carrying men and supplies. As night falls, you drop anchor and eat your K rations. You and your crew sleep on cots on the open deck of the LCM. At least you're safe—far from shore and near the transport carrier.

After six days at Normandy, you load the LCM onto a transport ship. You're headed back to the United States. Your commander has ordered you to Florida for advanced training on amphibious landing crafts. The war is still raging in the Pacific. You'll probably go there next.

By the end of 1944, France is free of German control. You helped make that happen.

THE END

To follow another path, turn to page 11.
To read the conclusion, turn to page 101.

You signal the coxswain, "Go!" The water is full of clothing, lost weapons, bodies, and even an overturned tank. The dark shadow you're seeing is probably just debris from earlier landings. After all, navy minesweepers cleared the area earlier.

But morning came before the minesweepers finished the job. When your LCM moves forward, it sets off a German mine that the minesweepers missed. It explodes. Steel balls and metal fragments spray the area. One hits you. You don't even have time to realize your mistake.

95

THE END

To follow another path, turn to page 11.
To read the conclusion, turn to page 101.

"I'll check it out," you say. You dive off the end of the ramp and search beneath the LCM until you find the obstacle. "It's a mine!" you yell as Tom helps you on board. The coxswain steers away, and the LCM safely delivers the wounded men to a troop carrier.

For the next few days, you carry supplies to shore. The army has moved on, and the beach is secure. The Germans are on the run.

German sailors planted mines that lay just below the water's surface, ready to detonate.

"You did well, men," Captain Orr says. "You played an important role in our victory."

Years later you tell your grandchildren about your experience in World War II. You tell them about the brave men who gave their lives on that faraway beach so that others could live in freedom.

97

THE END

To follow another path, turn to page 11.
To read the conclusion, turn to page 101.

You open the door. A German soldier peers back at you! You jump backward, and the German slams the door shut. You run to find an officer.

"There are no Germans left here," Lieutenant Blake scoffs.

"I'll bet you $5 there are," you say.

"You're on!" Lieutenant Blake bangs on the door. No answer. He fires a shot down a ventilation hole. Still no response. Finally he sends the soldiers for explosives and blows the door open. Fifteen German soldiers walk out. They're stunned by the blast but not hurt. Blake's men take the Germans prisoner.

Lieutenant Blake hands you a $5 bill. But the real prize comes later. You receive the Bronze Star for capturing 15 German prisoners of war.

THE END

To follow another path, turn to page 11.
To read the conclusion, turn to page 101.

The Germans are gone. There's no point in opening the door. Besides, it's time to return to the beach. When you get back, the LCM is repaired and ready to go. The next day you take more equipment to shore.

One day as you are loading a large gun onto the LCM, a cable breaks. It throws you into the ocean. Tom pulls you out of the water, but your leg is badly damaged. By the time you recover, the war has ended. You return home from the naval hospital full of stories of D-Day and your role in the amphibious navy.

THE END
To follow another path, turn to page 11.
To read the conclusion, turn to page 101.

The crewmen of the USS *Ward* showed off their scorecard of successful battles.

CHAPTER 5

A RECORD-BREAKING WAR

Navies played a major role in World War II. Sailors and Marines served on battleships, in submarines, and on the landing crafts that carried soldiers from ship to shore. Battles took place in the Atlantic and Pacific oceans, the Mediterranean Sea, and many smaller waterways.

One of the first major naval battles occurred in May 1941 when the German battleship *Bismarck* sank Great Britain's HMS *Hood*. The battle between the two giant ships lasted only 8 minutes before the *Hood* burned and sank.

The British fleet rushed to the scene. On the morning of May 27, British ships fired 2,800 shells at the *Bismarck*. Four hundred shells hit the target and destroyed the mighty ship. Only 116 of the 2,206 German sailors survived. British ships rescued 111. Those men became prisoners of war. German boats found five more survivors.

A few months later, on Sunday, December 7, 1941, the Japanese launched an attack on the U.S. Navy fleet at Pearl Harbor. Nearly 200 Japanese torpedo planes, bombers, and fighters fired on the U.S. battleships on Battleship Row. The attack surprised everyone.

The battleship *Arizona* was destroyed. The *Oklahoma* capsized. The *California*, *Nevada*, and *West Virginia* sank in shallow water. On the *Arizona*, 1,177 crewmen lost their lives. There were 2,403 Americans killed in the Pearl Harbor attack. Another 1,100 were injured. The next day the U.S. Congress declared war on Japan. The United States began fighting the Axis powers.

Meanwhile the Germans were gaining territory in Europe. France had fallen to the Germans. So had Norway, the Netherlands, and many other countries. The Allies wanted to land troops on the coast of Western Europe. British, Canadian, and American military leaders spent two years planning the invasion, called Operation Overlord. People would come to know it as D-Day.

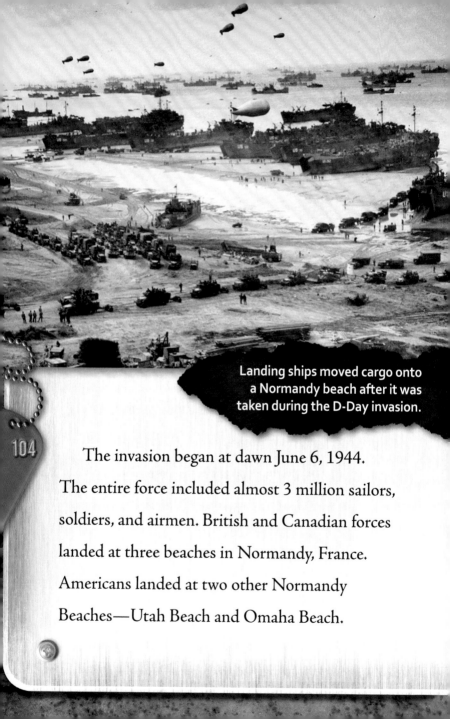

Landing ships moved cargo onto a Normandy beach after it was taken during the D-Day invasion.

The invasion began at dawn June 6, 1944. The entire force included almost 3 million sailors, soldiers, and airmen. British and Canadian forces landed at three beaches in Normandy, France. Americans landed at two other Normandy Beaches—Utah Beach and Omaha Beach.

More than 6,400 ships and landing craft brought 156,000 soldiers to the area. The sailors who operated the landing craft were key to the operation's success. The D-Day landing helped the Allies to victory. Germany surrendered on May 8, 1945.

The war in the Pacific continued for several more months. Many men who had served at Pearl Harbor or Normandy also served in the Pacific. World War II finally ended September 2, 1945, when Japan surrendered. Between 40 million and 50 million people were killed as a direct result of the conflict. No other war in world history has claimed more lives or spanned more territory than World War II.

TIMELINE

1939—Germany invades Poland September 1.

On September 3 Great Britain, France, Australia, and New Zealand declare war on Germany.

President Franklin D. Roosevelt declares the United States neutral September 5.

1940—Germany invades Norway and Denmark April 9.

On May 10 Germany invades France, the Netherlands, Belgium, and Luxembourg.

The Battle of Britain begins in July.

Roosevelt establishes a required draft in the United States September 16.

On September 27 Germany, Italy, and Japan unite as the Axis Powers.

1941—German battleship *Bismarck* sinks the British battleship *Hood* May 24.

On May 27 British ships destroy the *Bismarck*.

Japan bombs Pearl Harbor, Hawaii, December 7.

On December 8 the United States declares war on Japan.

1942—In spring the mass murder of Jews begins at Auschwitz concentration camp in Poland.

U.S. forces land on Guadalcanal in the Pacific August 7.

1943—Allies land in Sicily July 9–10.

Italy surrenders to the Allies September 3.

1944—On June 6 D-Day invasion begins at Normandy, France.

The Battle of the Bulge begins in France December 16.

1945—On February 19 U.S. forces land on Iwo Jima, off the coast of Japan.

The Allies reach Germany March 7.

On April 1 U.S. forces invade the Japanese island of Okinawa.

Germany surrenders to the Allies May 8.

The United States drops an atomic bomb on Hiroshima, Japan, August 6.

On August 9 the United States drops a second atomic bomb—this time on Nagasaki, Japan.

On September 2 Japan surrenders. World War II ends.

OTHER PATHS TO EXPLORE

In this book you've seen how the events of the past look different from three points of view. Perspectives on history are as varied as the people who lived it. Seeing history from many points of view is an important part of understanding it.

Here are some ideas for other World War II points of view to explore:

+ Navy nurses served on the hospital ships *Solace* and *Relief* to provide medical help to wounded sailors. What would it have been like to work in one of the floating hospitals?

+ During World War II the sailors of the U.S. Coast Guard not only guarded the U.S. coasts, but also went to war against German submarines. The U.S. Navy credited the Coast Guard with sinking or helping to sink 13 German submarines, called U-boats. What would it have been like to battle a German U-boat?

+ Serving on a submarine required special training and the ability to live in tight quarters beneath the sea. What would it have been like to spend weeks at a time underwater?

READ MORE

Dougherty, Steve. *Pearl Harbor: The U.S. Enters World War II*. New York: Franklin Watts, 2010.

Grove, Philip D., et al. *World War II: The War at Sea*. New York: Rosen Pub., 2010.

Konstam, Angus. *The Bismarck 1941: Hunting Germany's Greatest Battleship*. Oxford: Osprey Publishing, 2011.

Raum, Elizabeth. *World War II: An Interactive History Adventure*. Mankato, Minn.: Capstone Press, 2009.

INTERNET SITES

Use FactHound to find Internet sites related to this book. All of the sites on FactHound have been researched by our staff.

Here's all you do:

Visit *www.facthound.com*

Type in this code: 9781429647809

GLOSSARY

amphibious (am-FI-bee-uhs)—describes a type of vehicle or craft that can travel over land and also over or in water

brig (BRIGG)—where prisoners are held on a ship

hull (HUHL)—the frame or body of a ship

keel (KEEL)—the wooden or metal piece that runs along the bottom of a boat

mine (MINE)—small explosive device in the water or in the ground that is set off when a person steps on it or a vehicle moves over it

port (PORT)—the left side of a ship, facing forward

salvo (SAL-voh)—the release of bombs or other artillery from an aircraft

shell (SHEL)—a hollow cartridge filled with an explosive that will explode on contact with a target

starboard (STAR-burd)—the right side of a ship, facing forward

swastika (SWAH-stih-kuh)—a cross with bent arms used to represent the German Nazi party and its leader, Adolf Hitler

turret (TUR-it)—a rotating, armored structure that holds a weapon on top of a military vehicle

BIBLIOGRAPHY

Ballard, Robert D. *The Discovery of the Bismarck*. New York: Madison Publishing, 1990.

Forester, C. S. *Hunting the Bismarck*. London: Michael Joseph, 1959.

Gilbert, Martin. *The Second World War: A Complete History*. New York: Henry Holt, 1989.

Kennedy, David M., Ed. *The Library of Congress World War II Companion*. New York: Simon & Schuster, 2007.

La Forte, Robert S. and Ronald E. Marcello, Eds. *Remembering Pearl Harbor: Eyewitness Accounts by U.S. Military Men and Women*. Wilmington, Del.: SR Books, 1991.

Morison, Samuel Eliot. *The Two-Ocean War: A Short History of the United States Navy in the Second World War*. New York: Galahad, 1963.

North, Oliver. *War Stories II: Heroism in the Pacific*. Washington, D. C.: Regnery, 2004.

Stokesbury, James L. *A Short History of World War II*. New York: Perennial, 2001.

INDEX